General editor: Graham Handley

Brodie's Notes on Samuel Beckett's
Waiting for Godot

W. T. Currie BA

Pan Books London and Sydney

This edition published 1986 by Pan Books Ltd
Cavaye Place, London SW10 9PG
9 8 7 6 5 4 3 2 1
© W. T. Currie 1986
ISBN 0 330 50219 0
Photoset by Parker Typesetting Service, Leicester
Printed and bound in Great Britain by
Richard Clay (The Chaucer Press) Ltd, Bungay, Suffolk

Extracts are reprinted by permission of Faber and Faber Ltd
from *Waiting for Godot* by Samuel Beckett.

Performing rights in this play are controlled by Curtis Brown
Ltd, 162–168 Regent Street, London W1R 5TA.
Tel: 01-437 9700.

Contents

Page references in these Notes are to the Faber paperback edition of *Waiting for Godot,* but as both Acts are analysed separately in the textual notes and elsewhere, the Notes may be used with any edition of the play.

Preface

The intention throughout this study aid is to stimulate and guide, to encourage the reader's *involvement* in the text, to develop disciplined critical responses and a sure understanding of the main details in the chosen text.

Brodie's Notes provide a summary of the plot of the play or novel followed by act, scene or chapter summaries each of which will have an accompanying critical commentary designed to underline the most important literary and factual details. Textual notes will be explanatory or critical (sometimes both), defining what is difficult or obscure on the one hand, or stressing points of character, style or plot on the other. Revision questions will be set on each act or group of chapters to test the student's careful application to the text of the prescribed book.

The second section of each of these study aids will consist of a critical examination of the author's art. This will cover such major elements as characterization, style, structure, setting, theme(s) or any other aspect of the book which the editor considers needs close study. The paramount aim is to send the student back to the text. Each study aid will include a series of general questions which require a detailed knowledge of the set book; the first of these questions will have notes by the editor of what *might* be included in a written answer. A short list of books considered useful as background reading for the student will be provided at the end.

Graham Handley

The author and his work

Samuel Barclay Beckett was born on 13 April 1906 at Foxrock near Dublin, the second son of William Frank Beckett and May, *née* Roe. The family had few financial worries and lived in an imposing house, Cooldrinagh, facing the Wicklow mountains to the south of Dublin.

Beckett's mother appears to have suffered from tension head-aches arising from her desire to be a perfect mother and wife. During these periods of stress the whole household trembled and she herself retreated to her room. She also suffered from insomnia and spent many hours pacing the bedroom floor, where she had the floor-covering removed so that she could hear her own footfalls, however slight they may have been. Years later her son recalled this behaviour in his play *Footfalls*, and echoes it in his character, May.

The floor here . . . I say the floor here, now bare . . . once was carpeted, a deep pile. Till one night . . . she called her mother and said, Mother, this is not enough. . . . No, Mother, I must hear the feet, however faint they fall.

Beckett's father Bill, ostensibly a jolly person, had touches of cruelty in his character. This was shown in his demand for perfection from his sons and his equally strong demands as far as his wife's behaviour was concerned. Beckett himself nevertheless insists that his childhood was a happy one and that his parents did all they could to make it so.

Throughout their lives together, however, there was a com-plete clash of wills between Beckett and his mother. She was determined to dominate him; he was equally determined to remain his own person. He studiously avoided showing any of the expected emotions and seemed to be without fear. (One of his favourite games, for example, was to hurl himself from the high branches of a pine tree and trust that he would be caught safely in the lower reaches.) With this fearlessness went an inability to show affection or, at any rate, a determination to conceal such an emotion. On the other hand, the boys adored their father; this 'sweating, swearing, farting, belching red-faced mountain of a man' – a composite description derived from various of his acquaintances. Sadly he was too often absent from home to protect his children from the physical wrath of their mother.

After kindergarten and prep schools Beckett was entered at Portora Royal, Enniskillen, where he had a fine academic and sporting record. Earlier he had told his music teacher that what he wanted to do most was 'to play'. She was a little discomfited when he went on to make it clear that it was to play cricket for Ireland that he had in mind rather than mastering the piano.

Early in his academic career Beckett found himself grappling with the French language, as Earlsfort House School had been founded by Alfred Le Peton, who advertised himself as Professor of French and offered bilingual instruction even at that early age. The impeccable French accent used in the teaching at Earlsfort House was later to be dispelled by Beckett's French teacher at Portora, Miss Tennant. She had a strong Northern Irish accent, and to this day Beckett's French has a similar Irish sound. It was while he was at this school that the Easter Rebellion of 1916 broke out. The effect on his family was slight, though they watched the fires burning in Dublin. The whole affair was more a passing irritation than a serious disturbance, despite the fact that the establishment of the Free State was a consequence of the rising. Beckett, however, was haunted by the event and recalled it vividly years later. At Portora he lived the life of a normal public-school boy, but as he grew older he showed little affection for the place, not even responding to any of its Appeals. As the wife of the Headmaster in 1969 wrote in her information handout, when so many enquiries were being made about the new Nobel Prize winner: 'We can speak our pride in him, while he shows none in us.'

He did, nevertheless, maintain his interest in music while at Portora, and this balanced his sporting ability. Academically he was adequate and no more. For relaxation he played bridge and had a prodigious memory for the fall of the cards.

Beckett attended Trinity College, Dublin from 1923 to 1927. Here, from slightly mediocre beginnings, he found himself fourth in his year and received one of the much-sought-after Foundation Scholarships. He was strongly influenced by Professor Rudmose Brown, the Professor of French. He saw in Beckett his possible successor, and it was at his instigation that the author went to France in June 1926. Beckett's interest in France was further strengthened with the arrival at Trinity of Professor

Alfred Péron on an exchange visit from the École Normale Supérieure in Paris.

In 1927, when he took his degree, he was first in his year and received the large gold medal for outstanding scholarship. He was nominated exchange *lecteur* (Lecturer) at the École Normale, a post which he took up in October 1928. The gap was filled by a spell as a schoolmaster at Campbell College. This was a disaster for both the school and Beckett, and he withdrew at the end of the summer term before the contract was terminated by the outraged Headmaster.

At some time between 1928 and 1930 (when Beckett was a Lecturer at the École Normale in Paris) he first met James Joyce. In the years 1930–32 Beckett served four terms as Assistant Lecturer in French at Trinity College, Dublin, where the notorious production of *Le Kid* – a parody of Corneille's *Le Cid* – took place. A small annuity which he received in 1933, after the death of his father, became Beckett's basic means of livelihood until he was to receive the royalties from *Waiting for Godot* some twenty years in the future.

During World War II, in 1942, Beckett became a member of the French Resistance; he was later to be awarded the Croix de Guerre with gold star for work at this time. The citation read, 'Betrayed to the Germans, from 1943 he was forced to live clandestinely and with great difficulty.'

In November 1942 Beckett and Suzanne Deschevaux-Dumesnil, much later to be his wife, reached Roussillon in the region of the Vaucluse in south-east France, a section relatively free from German influence. Here he wrote *Watt*, probably the most autobiographical of his novels. Of it he said, 'Only a game, a means of staying sane, a way to keep my hand in.' The novel ends with the ambiguous statement: 'No symbols where none intended.'

Between 1946 and 1950 Beckett wrote the works by which he is best known and which will assure him a place in the histories of literature: the three novels, *Molloy*, *Malone Dies*, *The Unnameable*, and the play *Waiting for Godot* which was preceded by *Eleutheria*. (In 1950 his mother died.) The world première of *Waiting for Godot* took place in Paris on 5 January 1953 with director Roger Blin, and that of the English *Godot* in London on 3 August 1955. In 1959 Beckett was awarded an Hon.D.Litt by Dublin University; in 1969 he received the Nobel Prize for Literature.

To the present day Beckett has continued to write for stage, radio and television, but always with the strictest care over production. Pauses, movements, stage directions are all vital to him. Throughout, he has been consistent in the belief that the author's words are more important than the actor's interpretation. There is only one 'correct' version and that is Beckett's. Yet in *Catastrophe* (1982) we find him perhaps mocking himself – a gag is suggested for one of the characters and the Director says: 'This craze for explication! Every "i" dotted to death. Little gag! For God's sake!'

The importance of Beckett's life to an understanding of his work

Dr Duckworth, in his masterly introduction to Harrap's French edition of *Waiting For Godot*, makes the bold statement: 'Samuel Beckett's life is almost totally irrelevant to an understanding of his works.'

Beckett himself, by his own secluded habitation in Paris and the lowest of low profiles that he has maintained (apart from his appearances at the production of his plays), would seem to give weight to such an assertion. However, there are very obvious events and facts in his life that do throw some light on the interpretation of his work. It is important, for example, that he was born where he was, just outside Dublin, and yet alienated in some ways from the culture of that region by his Protestant background. The dominating personality of his mother had a disturbing effect on him, and yet he returned to his native land from his adopted one time and time again to see her. The period spent with Joyce and his family in Paris and the work he did for this fellow-Irishman could scarcely have left him untouched.

His time with the Resistance during the war filled Beckett's mind with new experiences and an awareness of danger and the closeness of death. His acceptance of an Honorary Degree from the University for which he ostensibly appeared to have little time is an example of the paradox of his personality. But the acceptance of the Nobel Prize for Literature by such a shy and reticent man is perhaps the greatest enigma in his character, despite the fact that he did not personally attend the presentation. All these aspects of his life are important to an understanding of his writing and cannot be brusquely dismissed.

The background to Beckett's work and its relation to *Waiting for Godot*

The history of the British theatre in the 1950s is exciting. Things were happening on the stage and in the minds of the playwrights that hadn't happened since the early stirrings of drama, when this form of expression was new.

For one thing, there were suddenly, it seemed, hundreds of new dramatists. Whereas formerly the art had been left to a few established and reliable writers, now the field was wide open. To cater for the new outpouring, small theatre clubs, more or less esoteric in nature, grew up and flourished or faded quickly, as support for them waxed or waned. Every kind of script was sent to these clubs, and every kind of label given to their work. These names varied from 'kitchen-sink' drama to 'the theatre of the absurd'. There certainly wasn't one label that fitted the whole gamut of plays. Theatre critics were bewildered by the situation, totally unsure of their ground and unwilling to risk too trenchant critical comment for fear that their own ignorance should be exposed. It is always interesting to look back at the critical comments made, by contemporaries, on any new genre. Every age has produced its gloriously wild statement about a play that has turned out to be a masterpiece a few generations ahead.

The main cause of bewilderment was that the old critical tenets of Aristotle and the ideas of a well-made play with carefully developed plot and character delineation no longer seemed to apply. The fall of a great man through some fatal flaw of character was no longer relevant. For one thing, there were no great men to be found in these plays. Here were tramps, misfits, outcasts from society, and they had already fallen as far as they could. Character seemed too fine a word to use of them, and they hardly appeared sufficiently universal to be symbols. The theatre no longer seemed a comfortable place to be. There were too many shocks, both to sensibility and to prejudice. If Bernard Shaw had stunned a generation of theatre-goers with his 'Not bloody likely!' in *Pygmalion*, here was shock a hundredfold greater. Pimps, panders and prostitutes were the new stage-walkers, and their language fitted their personalities.

There was a shift too of background. The complacent

suburban home with its middle-class standards was no longer sufficient to hold the attention of an audience that demanded, and got, stronger meat. Every aspect of life was looked at as closely as beneath a microscope, and unpleasant things were discovered under stones. Indeed, it is here that the dramatists are most held up to censure. It is all very well moving stones, but there must be some answer to the problems thus revealed. These young dramatists – for most of them were in their early twenties – asked plenty of questions, made many revelations, but did not appear to give any answers or suggest any remedies. It is not really sufficient for them to imply that their task is simply to point things out, and to leave the remedy to others.

There were still plays being written and produced with conventional constructions and comfortable plots, but perhaps a few critical comments from the time may help underline the general attitude to the new offerings:

'of a badness that must be called indescribable.' *The Times*
'a masterpiece of meaningless significance.' *Punch*
'another frightful ordeal.' *The Sunday Times*

These comments were made about Whiting's *Saint's Day*, Pinter's *The Birthday Party* and Arden's *Serjeant Musgrave's Dance* respectively. It has taken us nearly a quarter of a century to come to terms with this 'new' drama.

Looking back at that time, it is no wonder that students of modern drama find a new starting point in the small Théâtre Babylone on the Paris Left Bank. With *Waiting For Godot* (first published in the French language as *En attendant Godot* in 1952 by Les Éditions de Minuit), Beckett was to give them something that was quite new, something startling, yet acceptable to the extent that within a decade the play had become a classic in its own genre. This new convention of drama had been copied, parodied, translated and produced in a variety of forms and in a great number of languages. In its turn it had become established, though arguments about interpretation still raged. The truly remarkable thing was that opinion was not left to a few select people in avant-garde groups; the wider theatrical, and indeed the cinema-going, public had an opportunity to judge for itself.

Regarded dispassionately, the play seems far too obscure to have had so much time spent in attacking it, or in extolling its merits. Unless we study it closely, it appears to have been *concocted rather than planned*. Character and plots, as we have said, fly in the face of all that Aristotle demanded of them. The basic ingredient of any work of art appears to be lacking, so that communication itself is almost wilfully clouded. This holds not only between the author and ourselves but between the characters as well in their relationships with each other. There is an almost perverse desire to hide meaning in a welter of half-statements and stifled thoughts. A sound critical maxim, however, is *to be prepared to make the same intellectual effort to understand a work of imagination as the author did to compose it.* By following this advice here we may begin to be aware of the complex structure that faces us in the play. Perhaps we don't, in fact, have to go to such depths for full understanding, or it may be that, as with most works of real worth, there are different levels of awareness. Martin Esslin tells us that when a touring company acted *Waiting For Godot* before the prisoners of San Quentin gaol, San Francisco, they had no doubt about the real point of the play. They saw it as being about 'the release that never came'. They understood only too well the tedium of waiting and the promise that was never kept. So, basically, we have a *germinal* play, revolutionary in concept and startling in character. Tom Milne relates plays like it to the *théâtre maudit* of France, where only a few 'adventurous minds' will be prepared to make the effort to understand. Perhaps this may have been the case with the first audiences, but it is certainly not so now.

A more traditional modern dramatist, Christopher Fry, put the problem that must have faced Beckett quite clearly when he said, 'Two hundred years ago the dramatist knew how to approach the stage. Now the writer may find the lack of a universal manner a disadvantage.'

Subsequent dramatists have been taking whatever they found helpful from this play of Beckett's, rarely bothering even to acknowledge the debt. In our critical reading we will find as wide a variety of comment as we find plays within this modern period. The same mixture of styles that Shakespeare mocked is still with us, but Beckett has at least taught us not to look for narrative in our theatre. From the appearance of this play onwards, the idea of drama as action and story no longer applied. The writer had a new dimension to work in. Silence too was rediscovered as a positive quality, and we do not have to look far in *Godot* to see how Beckett exploits this in the attitudes of Vladimir and Estragon. In their movements of total silence these two scarecrows on the outer verge of humanity do rouse in us feelings of compassion. Robert Shaw underlines this when he says, 'Compassion's the thing. That's why I think I like *Waiting For Godot* more than anything I've seen since the war. I don't know why so many people call it a depressing play. Beckett writes about suffering in a way that makes me feel exhilarated – that I must get up and go out and do what I can.'

For one author at least, then, the message of the play is 'something must be done'. Finally, however, this message is the play itself.

Some interesting and illuminating precursors to *Waiting for Godot*

What shocked the early audiences in *Waiting For Godot* was its total unexpectedness. They were left floundering without terms of reference to aid them. Now, some thirty years later, that novelty has worn off, and we can look at the whole pattern of the play more objectively. When we study it today we see that a long tradition lay behind it, and the play came at the end of this tradition rather than at the beginning of a new train of thought. Hugh Venner, in *The Stoic Comedians*, gives us one line of thinking that may prove helpful. Just as T. S. Eliot's *The Waste Land* seems in some way totally new in its approach, yet in others it harks back to a long tradition of English literature (to Spenser and farther back to the Anglo-Saxons), so we see the same kind of pattern emerge in Venner's thesis.

Venner sees a development from Flaubert through Joyce and on to Beckett. Steeped as Beckett was in French literature, even to choosing that language for his own writing, such a theory has a sound foundation. A glance at Flaubert's *Bouvard et Pécuchet* (see *Further Reading*) will show many similarities to *Waiting For Godot*. On the very first page we have the meeting of the two men:

Two men appeared. One from the Bastille, the other from the Jardin des Plantes. The taller of the two, in a linen costume, walked with his hat pushed back, waistcoat undone and cravat in hand. The smaller one, whose body was enveloped in a brown frock-coat, had a peaked cap on his bent head.
When they came to the middle of the boulevard they both sat down at

the same moment on the same seat. Each took off his hat to mop his brow and put it beside him; and the smaller man noticed, written inside his neighbour's hat, Bouvard; while the latter easily made out the word Pécuchet, in the cap belonging to the individual in the frock-coat.

Once the recognition is completed, and note the importance of the hats in effecting it, we have an example of train-of-thought dialogue. Stock characters are brought on to the scene – a drunk man, a wedding party, a prostitute, a priest, and stock responses are forthcoming. These responses are developed in what would appear to be progressive conversation, but they are so predictable that the effect is rather like that of one musical instrument answered by another a note higher or lower.

Much later in *Bouvard et Pécuchet* we have a closer glimpse of the technique that Beckett uses in *Godot*. The friendship of the two men has come to a critical point; shall they part company or use the experience to draw closer together? The whole episode is analogous to a crisis in a marriage relationship.

Sometimes they opened a book and closed it again; what was the point? ... They yawned in front of each other, consulted the calendar, looked at the clock, waited for meals; and the horizon was always the same. Habits they had tolerated now upset them. Pécuchet became a nuisance with his mania for putting his handkerchief on the tablecloth; Bouvard's pipe was always in his mouth, and he swayed about as he talked ... When they were together they thought about different things.

This pair, too, are tightly bound and, despite feelings of irritation, each is unable to tear himself from the other.

Bouvard and Pécuchet have an insatiable and exhaustive thirst for knowledge. They are walking encyclopaedias. They search for the ultimate truth and even though it constantly eludes them they are prepared to set off on a new search. They never give up entirely, and like Vladimir and Estragon there is always hope, however faint. The notes to this unfinished book read:

So everything has come to pieces in their hands.
They have no interest left in life.
Each of them secretly harbours a bright idea. They hide it from each other. From time to time they smile when it occurs to them.
When they do eventually reveal their secret, it is that they shall return to their original job of copyists, so 'They go to work' after the construction of a double-sided desk. The wheel, in effect, has come full circle and they are back at their starting point.

Watt

'I began to write *Godot* as a relaxation from the awful prose I was writing at that time.' (Beckett) 'At that time', was the period of his 'exile' as an agricultural labourer in Avignon, 1942–1945. *Watt*, his last English novel, was the 'awful prose' he was writing, and in it we may find certain links with the later *Godot*. Beckett himself has pointed out some of these. Throughout the novel we have hints about the mysterious Mr Knott: 'But what do I know of Mr Knott? Nothing ... But what conception have I of Mr Knott? None.' Here we have the same kind of doubt and uncertainty that clouds our conception of Godot.

Watt makes much of the difficulty he encountered in his efforts to distinguish between what happened and what did not happen, between what was and what was not in Mr Knott's house. So, once again, we have the problem of reality and unreality; the actual and the imagined. Watt makes it perfectly clear that many things he describes as happening in Mr Knott's home either did not happen or happened quite differently from the way in which he describes them. Action and activity in the house are in a constant state of flux and there is no stability 'because all was a coming and a going.'

Watt's reminiscences are echoes of the activities of the tramps in *Waiting For Godot*. He remembers himself 'lying all alone, stone sober in the ditch, wondering if it was the time and the place.'

This comment is followed by two pages of text taken up by the incidence of the croaking of three frogs, with their individual calls of 'krak! krek! kirk!' Significant, too, is the fact that there are lines marking the pauses. Pauses and silences were to take a significant place in Beckett's stage productions and we do well to remember the importance he attached to them in *Godot*. Remember he even wanted to standardize them for every performance until persuaded that this would impose an impossible burden on the actors. There is even an incident in the novel connected with hats. A certain Mr Graves, as he relates his troubles to Watt, remains 'silent and expectant, floccilating (picking at) his hat.'

Apparently it was his habit to take his hat off, even in the open air, when he was talking to his betters. Oddly enough, in Scotland, and particularly on Clydeside in the shipyards, the hard-hat, i.e. the bowler hat, is a symbol of authority. Promotion is spoken of in such terms as, 'He's got the hard-hat.' Perhaps the same idea applied to the Ireland of Beckett's youth.

The closest analogy between *Watt* and *Godot*, however, is in the relationship of Watt to Mr Knott. There is the same hint of fearfulness that we have with the tramps; a desire to meet Godot but an underlying fear of the encounter. Watt cannot be sure whether he is glad or sorry not to see Mr Knott more often. In one way he wishes to meet Knott face to face but in another he was glad not to, because 'He feared to do so.'

There is this same element of fear in Vladimir and Estragon. Watt is concerned with the relationship between a certain Erskine, who lived in the house, and Mr Knott, and wonders how they conversed or if indeed they ever did. He comes to the conclusion that they conversed in undertones; the undertones of master and servant. Perhaps there is here something of the relationship of Pozzo and Lucky and the subsequent reversal of their roles, in *Waiting For Godot*.

Later there is an accident when Watt puts his foot through the slats of a rustic bridge, Watt and the narrator of the story then set about repairing it, each from his own end and lying full length on their stomachs. When they eventually meet – 'then we did a thing we seldom did, we embraced' – after the manner of Vladimir and Estragon.

If we seek a clue to Lucky's tirade of words in *Waiting For Godot* we find a hint of it in Watt's manner of speaking. It is compared to the mumbling of the Mass or a man in delirium. In its disregard of the rules of grammar or syntax it is most reminiscent of Molly Bloom's famous soliloquy at the end of James Joyce's *Ulysses*. What could be more like Lucky's manner of speaking than, 'Watt spoke as one speaking to dictation, or reciting, parrot-like, a text, by long repetition became familiar'?

Mercier et Camier

Perhaps *Mercier et Camier*, written in 1946 and not published until 1970, gives us the greatest insight into the world of Vladimir and Estragon. Beckett thought that the novel was over autobiographical and did not work as fiction because he had too much of himself in it. The two heroes, Mercier and Camier, have many of the traits of the later two in *Waiting for Godot*. They are Beckett's earliest vaudeville couple and, indeed, the first of their encounters is stage-managed in the way of a music-hall turn. There is ambiguity right from the start:

Camier was first to arrive . . . In reality Mercier had forestalled him . . . Not Camier, then, but Mercier was first to arrive.'

So we have a situation turning back on itself and the opposite of what is said at the beginning is posited at the end of the episode. The author goes on to present a table of arrivals and departures where each misses the other by sometimes five and at other times ten minutes.

We have a haunting echo of the meeting place of Vladimir and Estragon in the rendezvous of these two. They first meet in a square which is dominated by a tree – a huge copper-beech, but it is a tree in decay which will '. . . rot till finally removed bit by bit'.

The use of *stichomythia* (rapid interchange of dialogue) is clear from their first exchange. Monosyllables are spat out like machine-gun fire:

Let us go home
Why?
It won't stop all day
Long or short . . .

and the whole passage is written without quotation marks.

Doubt and uncertainty cloud every aspect of their meeting. Even when a notebook is consulted the conclusion is gloriously inconclusive: 'We shall never know at what hour we arranged to meet today, so let us drop the subject.'

The need for some external agent to spur them into action is emphasized in the episode with the park keeper. This character arrives on the scene with fatuous questions about dogs and bicycles (an echo of Beckett's life in Dublin). To his questions Mercier says: 'Can it, I wonder, be the fillip we needed to get us moving?'

But, before moving, there must be thought and the suggestion of sustenance: 'What about a bite to eat, said Camier. Thought first, said Mercier, then sustenance.' The long debate that follows is broken by longer silences. Once more we are reminded of Beckett's preoccupation with the controlled pause and the pregnant silence.

The first chapter of the novel ends with the kind of forlorn optimism we have in *Waiting For Godot*. Mercier sees some hope for the future and believes that, perhaps, 'all will be in order at last.'

Camier accepts this pious hope with the politest of replies: 'That will be delightful.'

So, there was a considerable body of writing, some published, much unpublished, behind Beckett when he came to write *Godot*, but its publication did not mean that he was simply going over old ground. It is true that as a consistent writer Beckett teases at the same thought and returns to similar themes again and again, but he invariably deals with them from a slightly different angle. There is always some progression and development, however slight. But the main difference, however, between *Waiting For Godot* and the earlier prose works is that the play lacks a narrator. We, the audience, take his place and assist, as it were, in the difficulties Estragon and Vladimir suffer in the vital matter of communication. Whereas the novel can advance in a positive way, the play must of necessity remain static and the actors be fixed on stage for the whole performance.

Plot

There is virtually no plot in *Waiting For Godot*: it could perhaps best be described as the dilemma of two characters. Beckett has placed his two tramps (or clowns) in a situation from which there is no escape, unless through the mind. They are tied to the one place, reduced to the basics of human need and incapable of positive action as individuals, so dependent are they on each other. They are not even able to fetch a rope for their own suicide, for that would imply a separation which they cannot face. When they do part for short spells their reunion is touching, almost painful.

It is the escape through suicide that is given most prominence in the play. They have tried it before, and thought about it often. Towards the end of Act 1, as they think about fetching a piece of rope for hanging themselves, Estragon remarks, 'Do you remember the day I threw myself into the Rhône?' and Vladimir replies, 'That's all dead and buried ... There's no good harking back on that.'

The attempt to escape through suicide at the end of Act 2 is no more successful. The cord which holds up Estragon's trousers isn't strong enough.

They each take an end of the cord and pull. It breaks. They almost fall.

So they continue to wait, and we are left to resolve their dilemma in our own way. The author demands that we share their situation with them; we cannot simply ignore it, for we are part of it. As John Donne wrote, 'No man is an island entire of itself.'

Act summaries, critical commentaries, textual notes and revision questions

As long ago as 1953 Raymond Williams commented on the simplicity of the everyday speech used in *Waiting for Godot*. As we are dealing with relatively basic people the speech, for the most part, follows that pattern and is reasonably straightforward. Every so often, however, we have some of the verbal juggling that we find in the words of James Joyce, and there are deeper ideas lurking behind the surface meanings. The commentary and textual notes which follow may be of some assistance.

Act 1

We meet Estragon sitting on a mound wrestling with his boots when Vladimir enters. The two have been parted and it would appear that Vladimir had feared that this parting was permanent. They discuss their earlier attempts at suicide including the idea of jumping from the top of the Eiffel Tower. But they realize that in their present state they would not even be allowed admittance to the Tower. Repentance is discussed and reference made to the Bible. The theme of the two thieves sharing the Crucifixion is introduced by Vladimir and rounded off with the disparaging comment that people as a whole are gullible.

The reason for their present situation, where they are and why they are, is now made clear. They are waiting for Godot. Once more they return to the thought of suicide, and hanging from the tree as the means. They decide to wait till Godot comes, and fall silent as they think they hear him approaching on horseback. With that Pozzo appears and, far at the end of a rope, Lucky. Pozzo eats his picnic and Estragon asks for the leavings. The tramps remonstrate against Lucky's harsh treatment. They are intrigued as to why the servant doesn't lay down his burden. Pozzo makes a virtuoso performance of preparing his reply, complete with throat spray. Lucky, apparently, wants to impress him, for fear of being dismissed. This further encourages the sympathy of the tramps, but a kick from Lucky at Estragon suggests that their pity might be misplaced. However, the tramps still harp on the indignity and iniquity of Lucky's lot, and Pozzo's intention of selling him at the fair, after so many years of faithful service. Pozzo loses his pipe. The three of them discuss the themes of night, the passing of time and the waiting. Pozzo offers some diversion from Lucky in the way of philosophy or song and dance. This leads to the breathless and lengthy speech of the unhappy slave. This is brought to an abrupt end by the seizure of his hat which seems to have taken on the same mysterious powers as the conch in Golding's *Lord of the Flies*. Without it he is speechless. Pozzo and Lucky depart and the tramps discuss the diversion and the identity of the two recent guests. It is implied that they may have met previously. A small boy enters with the message that Godot will come on the morrow. The tramps discuss parting from each other, but inertia keeps them from any positive action.

In Beckett's writing the stage-directions are as important as the dialogue, so straightaway we have the pathos of Estragon struggling to take off his boots. Note the irony of 'admiringly' when Estragon tells Vladimir that he has been asleep in a ditch.

a little heap of bones That is, dead. Note the dependence of man on man.

blathering Talking nonsense, babbling. Note the force of the word.

I'd like to hear . . . what I have Vladimir has a condition caused, probably, by enlargement of the prostate gland. It makes it difficult for him to control his urination.

AP-PALLED The division of the word is deliberate, with its connotation with 'pall' and 'hearse'.

repented A word underlining one of the themes of the play.

privation The condition of being without something formerly or properly possessed.

from ear to ear i.e. like a clown.

that's where we'll go for our honeymoon Who? Later when the two talk of parting it is rather as though a marriage is breaking up.

You should have been a poet The irony of this is underlined by Estragon's indicating his rags.

the two thieves The two who were to be crucified with Jesus.

Gogo, return the ball So the dialogue is regarded as a game.

And is it Saturday? The suggestion is that time is meaningless.

The English say, cawm An Irishman making fun of what his countrymen consider English affectation. Here is a sustained example of music-hall cross-talk.

bawd Woman in charge of the girls in a brothel.

pugilist Fist-fighter.

Silence Note how frequently this is used in the stage-directions.

Where it falls mandrakes grow It was a belief that when a man was hanged he ejaculated, and where the sperm fell a mandrake would grow. The mandrake, through its forked shape was likened to the human, particularly the male, form. The plant was thought to have magical properties, and shrieked like a human when pulled from the ground.

Bough not break Note the baby talk and the nursery-rhyme rhythm.

To strike the iron before it freezes Reversal of the actual proverb 'to strike while the iron is hot'.

supplication Prayer, plea. Very educated language for a tramp.

to assert his prerogatives They no longer have rights or prerogatives. There is irony and bitterness in the remark.

The winds in the reeds Perhaps the reference is to the *Morte d'Arthur* of Tennyson or *La Belle Dame Sans Merci* of Keats.

Carrot Association back to the horse they think they have heard.

vacuously Without any expression.

The essential doesn't change This is what they both want, and what mankind wants, stability.

A terrible cry, close at hand Shock and drama – something is about to happen.

Pozzo drives Lucky by means of a rope Horse and carrot, reward and punishment association.

trying to remember the name Note the confusion over identity. What does it tell us about the nature of reality?

The mother had the clap Note how quickly the association with VD follows with 'We're not from these parts, sir.'

Let's say no more about it . . . Up hog! Here we have the sadistic treatment of his servant and the Dictator in embryo.

voraciously Greedily.

What ails him Archaic language, again reminiscent of Keats in *La Belle Dame Sans Merci*.

chafing Rubbing that causes soreness.

slaver Saliva issuing from the mouth.

cretin Person with deformity and mental retardation caused by thyroid deficiency.

goitre Enlargement of the thyroid gland in the throat, shown as a prominent neck swelling. Note here how all the physical sides of Lucky are expressed as being distasteful.

grampus A spouting, blunt-headed, whale-like dolphin.

to cod me To 'take me in', to fool me.

in his shoes . . . his due Note the clichés in this speech.

The tears of the world are a constant quantity An almost biblical utterance – like 'the poor are always with us'. Sadness is for all times and all places.

knook (Fr. *un knouk*) A word invented by Beckett. According to Professor Colin Duckworth, it was formed on the analogy of the

Russian word knout, a whip or knotted rope.

He consults his watch Yet what he really needs is a diary or a calendar.

Crucify him like that Biblical connotation once more.

dudeen Irish for short clay tobacco pipe.

Time has stopped Significant in a play that concerns itself so much with time and its nature.

Adam Estragon when asked his name replies, 'Adam'. He thus sees himself as the Father of Mankind, the first of men. Or he is parrying the question as Ulysses hid his identity under the name of Noman.

farandole A lively dance of Provençal origin.

fling Impetuous dance, as in 'Highland Fling'.

fandango A Spanish-American dance in triple time.

aesthete Someone highly sensitive towards the arts.

pulverizer A machine for reducing stone etc to dust and powder. Note Estragon's joke about his lungs – as though they act independently.

Wait The key to the play repeated by the three of them. Note the stage comment before Lucky's tirade. Pozzo, presumably, has heard it before and knows that much of it is directed against him. Vladimir and Estragon are eventually overwhelmed and frightened by it. All three strive violently to bring it to an end.

apathia Stoicism, freedom from emotion.

athambia Astonishment, fearlessness.

aphasia Lack of the faculty of speech, as a result of brain damage.

the divine Miranda Prospero's daughter in Shakespeare's *The Tempest*.

Acacacacademy of Anthropopopometry Anthropometry is a science based on human measurement.

Essy-in-Possy *In esse*, being alive. *In posse*, potential, possible.

alimentation Nourishment.

defecation Disposal of waste, body-matter: excretion.

camogie Irish hurling.

Bishop Berkeley (1685–1755) He postulated that if God does not exist, the existence of the universe itself and of mankind is very doubtful.

Steingweg and Peterman Lucky is probably referring to Heinrich Engelhard Steinway (originally Steinweg) 1797–1871, German-born American piano maker; and August Petermann (1822–78), a cartographer of Gotha, Germany.

penicilline and succedanea Of the type penicillin, the antibiotic able to prevent the growth of certain disease-causing bacteria, or its substitute, a thing to fall back on in default of the real drug.

water ... fire ... air ... earth Lucky is naming the Four Elements: Earth, Air, Fire and Water.

half-hunter A watch, generally of gold. Demi-hunter: a watch having a hunting case, with a hole in the lid permitting the time to be told when the lid is closed.

fob Small pocket for watch in waistband of trousers.

I mind the goats, sir ... He minds the sheep, sir Like Cain and his brother Abel (Genesis, 4, 1–16).

The moon rises Note the symbolism of the moon with, perhaps, a hint
 of Lady Gregory's play, *The Rising of the Moon*.
Pale for weariness Another echo of Keats? 'Alone and palely loitering'
 from *La Belle dame Sans Merci*.
crucified quick Pun on 'quick', living; crucifixion is a slow death.
grape-harvesting A recall of Beckett's earlier time in France.

Revision questions on Act 1

1 What is the significance of the mention of the Eiffel Tower at
this point in the play, and later in the Act?

2 What difference do you find in the tramps' approach to the
Bible in this scene? What significance do you see in this?

3 Why do you think Vladimir is so adamant about not being
told Estragon's dream?

4 List the qualities of Lucky that reduce him to the level of an
animal.

5 Describe the appearance of Lucky from comments made by
others about him and from the stage directions.

6 Follow closely the change in attitude of Vladimir and
Estragon towards Pozzo.

7 What reason does Pozzo put forward for Lucky's not putting
down his luggage? Do you think this is the real reason?

8 What is the significance of Pozzo's description of the sky at
this point in the play? Look closely at the speech, and attempt a
critical appraisal.

9 What do you think Lucky is trying to say in his long speech?
Make an attempt to comment on its dramatic significance.

10 What is the dramatic purpose of the entrance of the
messenger boy at the end of the Act?

Act 2

The next day, at the same place and time as Act 1. Vladimir's
cyclical song starts the scene. Estragon enters and upbraids his
companion for having let him leave. There follows discussion

about the consequences of their [brief] separation which vary between consolation and utter desolation, then follows the tale of Estragon's treatment by the unknown ones. The two friends try to recall the events of the previous day. Memory takes them farther back to the seemingly inconsequential Macon country [until we remember Beckett's sojourn in France with Suzanne and his time with the Resistance]. Then there ensues a long dialogue concerned with the nature of life and existence, based on the ability to think – *Cogito ergo sum.* Something positive has occurred, at any rate as regards the tree: it has sprouted leaves. Estragon tries to excuse his lack of boots, but they are where he left them, under the tree. The boots, it appears, are a positive sign of the tramps' existence.

Sleep follows as a palliative to their situation and is a means for Vladimir to show tenderness and compassion in his treatment of Estragon. He is like a mother calming a child's night fears. Lucky's hat is now seen as a proof of the previous day's happenings. This confirms both location and existence once more. Then follows the hat routine used by so many comedians. They further try to confirm reality as children do by a miming game of pretending to be Lucky and Pozzo, but this ends with the hysteria of discovery when they think that Godot is indeed upon them and, like Adam and Eve, they have nowhere to hide from his wrath. Another game of invective ensues, rising to the climax (or descending to the depth) of the word 'Critic'. This leads to the ecstasy of making-up the quarrel.

After further miming, culminating in the impersonation of the tree itself, they are shocked back to reality by the arrival of Pozzo and Lucky. The dramatic change in these two leads to a further reversal of roles, where it now seems the tramps have a dominating upper hand. Pozzo, grovelling, offers payment for their help, and the tramps make as though to give assistance. Some time passes before any definite action to help is taken, and they are shocked to hear that Pozzo is now blind. The tramps use their discovery to expand further their ideas about time. Pozzo himself suggests that ideas of duration are of little consequence to the blind. At last Pozzo remembers his servant, and Estragon is sent, rather reluctantly after his previous encounter, to look for him. Now the roles are reversed with a vengeance as Estragon puts the boot into the prostrate Lucky. To balance the blindness of Pozzo it now seems that Lucky is dumb. Pozzo rounds on the pair of them for the constant torments about time, and Lucky and he continue on their hazardous journey with the sound of their falling off stage.

The boy messenger appears and addresses Vladimir as Mr Albert. He denies having been there the previous day. Vladimir questions him about the appearance and nature of Mr Godot. Enraged by the vagueness of his reply, Vladimir makes a rush at the boy who retreats in terror. Estragon wakes from his semi-conscious state, and the two again contemplate suicide by hanging from the tree. The final piece of clowning – an aspect of production insisted on by Beckett – leads to the last tableau. The rope to be used for the hanging is the string from Estragon's trousers; it proves too weak and the trousers fall to the ground. We are left with the poignant sight of the two tramps still unable to take any positive steps to depart.

The tree has four or five leaves Note this stage direction; something has changed – the tree has sprouted these few leaves.

A dog came in . . . till he was dead This first stanza of Vladimir's song probably refers to Lucky.

There were ten of them Exaggeration after the manner of Shakespeare's Falstaff. Estragon's fantasy.

oozes . . .pus Both connote putrefaction and decay.

Calm yourself Remember the fun made in Act 1 of the English pronunciation.

Macon country Beckett is here remembering his own wartime stay in France.

puked Vomited.

can't think of the name of the man In the French text he is Bonnelly who, when told he was in a play by Beckett, couldn't understand why as he'd scarcely spoken to him.

All the dead voices An echo of T. S. Eliot's 'The Hollow Men'.

VLADIMIR: Help me! A poignant cry from the heart.

charnel-house Repository for dead bodies.

In a single night . . . single night Note the wonderment expressed by the repetition.

In another compartment As if they are making a journey by rail or as if life can be broken into fragments of time.

Pull up your trousers Vladimir and Estragon clown over pulling up the trousers to show the wound.

Pig [And later **Hog**] The words echo Pozzo and his domineering tone.

Boots The implied suggestion that the Boy took them links us with Act 1.

foetal Like a child in the womb. The references which follow are all about reversion to childhood.

coquettishly Like a girl flirting light-heartedly.

mannequin Woman employed by dressmaker to display clothes by wearing them.

Gonococcus Micro-organism causing gonorrhoea.

Spirochaete Spiral-shaped bacterium causing syphilis.

Punctilious Strict in the observance of detail.

Morpion Estragon seems to have concocted this word in order to keep up the dialogue.

Crritic The greatest of the insults. In the French version the word is 'Architect' – because of the destruction of old buildings.

ballocksed A favourite Irish expression meaning, roughly, in dire straits, in real trouble.

In anticipation of some tangible return Officialese or 'gobbledygook'.

congeners Persons or things nearly related or similar to another.

aphoristic An aphorism is a short, pithy statement expressing a general truth sometimes ironic as in the case of Sir Toby Belch, hiding in *Twelfth Night* and overhearing Malvolio when he observes, 'Some are born great' etc.

crablouse Parasitical insect infecting the human body.

Look at the little cloud There seems to be no point in this statement until we remember 1 Kings, 18, 43–44 with Elijah on Mount Carmel: 'And (Elijah) said to his servant, Go up now, look towards the sea. And he went up, and looked, and said, There is nothing. And he said, Go again seven times. And it came to pass at the seventh time, that he said, Behold there ariseth a little cloud out of the sea like a man's hand . . .' It is probably the repetition of the servant's mission that is important here. The whole passage refers to the contest between Jehovah and Baal. Elijah's mocking is revealing: 'You'll have to shout louder than that to catch the attention of your god! Perhaps he is talking to someone, or has gone aside to relieve himself, or maybe he is away on a journey, or is asleep and needs to be wakened!' Not unlike the Godot in the play. Note, too, Joyce's short story in *Dubliners*, 'The Little Cloud'.

Perhaps he can see into the future Tiresias or another prophet saw the goddess Pallas Athene bathing, and was splashed with water and blinded. Later the goddess repented and gave him the power of soothsaying.

highwaymen Slightly anachronistic in the context.

repertory Theatrical performance of various plays for short periods by one company.

caryatids A caryatid is a female figure used in a stone column and for support.

Wonderful! Wonderful, wonderful sight! Note Pozzo's use of irony.

Memoria praeteritorum bonorum Remembering happy days that have passed.

They give birth astride a grave The shortness of life.

Revision questions on Act 2

1 What is the importance of Estragon's boots at this point?

2 What has happened to Estragon between the Acts? Consider the evidence carefully in your answer.

3 Follow the steps in Vladimir's attempt to remind Estragon of what happened the previous day.

4 Trace the development of the thought that leads Estragon to say, 'That wasn't such a bad little canter.'

5 What is the importance of Lucky's hat in this Act?

6 Consider the function of the mimes performed by Vladimir and Estragon in this Act.

7 Explain what Vladimir means by, 'In anticipation of some tangible return'. How do the tramps go about getting this 'tangible return'?

8 What does Estragon mean when he says of Pozzo, 'He's all humanity'?

9 What significance is there in the tramps' treatment of Lucky? Why do you think it changes?

10 What is the dramatic significance of the entry of the Boy in this Act?

Beckett's art in *Waiting for Godot*
The characters

The enigma of Godot

Beckett's play has gained universal recognition as the one in which the title character never appears. It is not surprising, therefore, that many attempts have been made to identify Godot and to elucidate the mystery of the play.

The author himself when asked who Godot was said enigmatically, 'If I knew I would have said so in the play', the implication behind the statement being that he has done just that, and made clear who or what Godot was. Godot's non-arrival provides the only fact about him in the whole play, though we do learn certain things about him.

The tramps see him as being able to give them comfort. They look forward to being taken to his farm and being cared for. The impression is that he is paternalistic, almost patriarchal, like the God of the Old Testament, meting out punishment and reward. His beard (which, according to the messenger may be white) adds to this impression of him. We may even picture him as portrayed by William Blake in one of his etchings. He does seem to have the human failing of favouritism, as he beats one of the messengers but not the other. Through their occupations he seems to divide the sheep from the goats, again a strong echo from the Old Testament. He is obviously a figure to be feared, as the tramps constantly cower at his impending approach, and there is no doubt that there is an element of the judge in him.

However much we may play with linguistics and phonetics and point out that the play was first written in French, and the emphasis of pronunciation therefore would have fallen on the second syllable of the name, we still have sympathy with the critic who forthrightly solved the problem: 'Godot – is God'. Over-simplified as such a solution may be, we cannot deny that there is much of the Deity in him.

Perhaps it is as well for us to take what meaning we want from the character, and to have our own ideas about the person of Godot. The author has every right to point to the work itself as his solution of the puzzle.

Vladimir

When I think of it ... all these years ... but for me ... where would you be ... ?

Vladimir is the dominating personality. He takes his responsibility for Estragon seriously: 'It's too much for one man' (p.10), and he voices the text of the sermon of the play: One of the thieves was saved. It is through him that we follow the idea of salvation as a theme. He is the religious one, the seeker after truth; while Estragon contents himself with the pictures and colourful maps of his Bible (p.12), Vladimir ponders its philosophy and religious message. Estragon, almost wilfully stupid, serves as a foil, a foolish child for whom everything must be reduced to its simplest terms. He dismisses the idea of salvation and the universal obtuseness with which the idea is received: 'People are bloody ignorant apes' (p.13), although he seems to be one of them. When the tramps contemplate splitting up Vladimir has scant hope for Estragon's survival or determination to strike out on his own. It is to Vladimir that Estragon cries plaintively like a child when he is disturbed suddenly from sleep; it is to him also, as the provider, that Estragon looks for food. As the father-figure he is expected to provide the answer to any perplexing question:

Vladimir: How do you mean tied?
Estragon: Down.
Vladimir: But to whom. By whom?
Estragon: To your man.
Vladimir: To Godot? Tied to Godot? What an idea!

'No question of it. (*Pause*) For the moment' (pp.20–21). There is special significance in the fact that Estragon calls Godot 'your man', as though the sole responsibility for their waiting rests on Vladimir. Nor must we miss the importance of Vladimir's 'For the moment.'

When Pozzo and Lucky first appear it is Vladimir who proves himself the man of action. Estragon plucks him back from going to Lucky's aid when he falls; later he is the first to show compassion for Lucky's treatment and condition (p.27). Later still he finds the presence of Pozzo distasteful, and it is now his turn to make the suggestion, 'Let's go', and Estragon who holds him back with 'We're in no hurry' (p.28).

When we reach the point of Lucky's entertainment it is

Vladimir who prefers the intellectual diversion: 'I'd like well to hear him think' (p.39). Vladimir, by putting the hat back on Lucky's head, seems to set free the spate of words which issues forth in his long, quasi-philosophical oration. Indeed, it is only when the headgear is removed that Lucky relapses into his accustomed silence. Vladimir takes the initiative in the conversation with the Boy, though Estragon foresees nothing but complications. There is no doubt, however, that it is Mr Albert, the name to which Vladimir responds, who is being sought out by Godot's messenger. He also retains a note of optimism near the end of Act 1 when he tells Estragon: 'Tomorrow everything will be better' (p.52). When that tomorrow comes it is he who recalls the events of the previous day and recapitulates for Estragon and the audience the actions of Pozzo and Lucky.

In Act 2 Vladimir once more serves as comforter to the frightened Estragon as he awakens from a nightmare-ridden sleep. Previously he has fed him, this time with a more exotic root, a radish, which has not been to Estragon's liking. Again in this Act it is Vladimir who first shows compassion, though this time it is for Pozzo, who is now blind, but Estragon still thinks that Godot himself has arrived.

Faced by a new situation when they can be of some help, Vladimir grasps the opportunity: 'Let us do something, while we have the chance! It is not every day that we are needed' (p.79). It is predictable that their efforts to help will be frustrated in a tangle of fallen bodies.

Just before the final arrival of the Boy, Vladimir makes a despairing attempt to rationalize their situation, and introduces the startling image of birth astride an open grave, thereby telescoping the whole of man's life into a very brief span indeed. This time it is he who recognizes the moment of challenge with 'Off we go again', as he greets Godot's messenger boy. He too is given the last word about salvation, his personal theme (p.94).

Estragon

'Beat me, certainly they beat me.'

From the start he seems doomed to suffer. It would appear that Estragon somehow provokes hostility by his unthinking actions, and Vladimir feels that he could avert retaliation by dealing with first causes. Throughout the play Estragon seeks escape in sleep, but is always ushered back to stark reality and seeks comfort from Vladimir. Yet often it is the latter who denies him the rest he needs.

It is his childish logic that prevents their first attempt at suicide by hanging from the bough of the barren tree. He realizes that he, being the lighter, will probably succeed, and that consequently Vladimir, the heavier, will break the bough, survive and be left lonely. In the encounter with Pozzo he is quick to deny any acquaintance with Godot. Although he is such a timid creature, he is not averse to asking Pozzo for the chicken bones, and much of his time is taken up with requests for food. Like Kipling's Kim, he is prepared to let anyone acquire merit by helping him to charity, whether it be Vladimir or Pozzo. Similar helpful action on his part does not seem to be so successful, and a bruised shin seems to be his only reward for going to wipe Lucky's tears. Not surprisingly there is an Irish exaggeration about 'I'll never walk again!' as he nurses his leg (p.32).

Estragon shows his first aggressive tendency in his conversation with the Boy – here he is at his most forcible: 'Approach when you're told, can't you?' When he shakes the Boy's arm Vladimir orders him to let the latter alone; Estragon's only excuse is, 'I'm unhappy'.

It is Estragon who makes an unprovoked attack on Lucky – though Vladimir fully concurs (p.88) – when he is lying inert and unable to defend himself. It is only the pain this gives him in his own foot that makes Estragon stop. He resorts to his cure for all ills – sleep – and on being wakened once more by Vladimir protests yet again, 'Why will you never let me sleep?' (p.89).

Just before the end of the play it is Estragon who, perhaps unwittingly, suggests the answer to their dilemma. Godot has again failed to materialize, and he says:

'And if we dropped him?' (*Pause*) 'If we dropped him?' (p.93).

But it is no use, there is no answer here after all:

Vladimir: 'He'd punish us.'

It is to Estragon that the last chance of action is given in the play: 'Yes, let's go.' The stage direction, *They do not move*, clearly shows that they are bound to the wheel of time and the cycle is about to commence once more.

Pozzo and Lucky

These two are inextricably bound together. They act and react on each other in a special way. We see Lucky first, laden with luggage and tethered by a rope. His condition certainly belies his name, for he is driven by Pozzo, who is still in the wings when the rope is at full stretch. Apart from the luggage, the whip is the main prop at this point in the play.

Pozzo expects to be recognized by the two tramps, and quickly catches up the name of Godot, for whom Estragon at least has mistaken him. It transpires that he owns the land on which they are waiting. There is a great deal of stage business while Pozzo settles himself to his picnic; this gives the tramps an opportunity to inspect Lucky, who gives the impression of an overworked horse. The rope has caused a running sore on his neck, but he is 'not bad looking', as Vladimir points out (p.25). They are unsuccessful in getting any response from him other than the prolonged stare he gives Estragon at the request for the chicken bone. Pozzo makes great play of the tramps' waiting for Godot; he toys with the name as his own name has already been played with, and stuns Vladimir with his suggestion that Godot has their future in his hands. How has he come to such a conclusion on so little evidence? Is he in Godot's confidence?

There is a subtle change of relationship between the protagonists at this point, which does not go unnoticed by Pozzo. The tramps, deferential and fearful as we saw them at the first encounter, are now emboldened to ask a question as equals, and it is remarked that no good will come of this. Pozzo prepares to answer the question put to him about Lucky in the manner of the most temperamental prima donna, and shows all the attributes of the professional politician. He strikes a pose, and waits to become the full of focus of attention. Like many another public speaker, he loses his train of thought and has to be prompted by Vladimir and Estragon, who mime the plight of Lucky. We reach the nub of the relationship between these two when Pozzo says, 'Remark that I might just as well have been in his shoes and he in mine' (p.31). We are soon made aware, however, of Pozzo's dependence on his servant, and the debt he owes him (p.33).

In an emotional outburst we learn of Pozzo's suffering at the hands of Lucky and his need to be rid of him, but he is able to regain control, and we are left wondering whether indeed, considering their roles, the master can be made to suffer at the hands of the servant.

As a reward for their civility and patience the tramps are to be beguiled by a dance and an oration from Lucky. The one is as short as the other is long and breathless. This is Lucky's great virtuoso moment, and he turns himself on and off like a tap. Theatrically the effect is as startling as the shock of white hair which appears when he takes off his hat, or the contrasting baldness of Pozzo when he removes his headgear. The scene ends with the exaggerated civilities of leave-taking and the continued dominance of Pozzo over his slave.

In the second Act the roles of the two are as before, but Pozzo in his blindness is more deeply dependent on Lucky. The bully has lost much of his arrogance, and now looks for pity. The tramps consider the possibility of going to Pozzo's aid, unaware, apparently, that he is blind. They accept this fact without comment when they are told, as they accept everything that happens to them without question.

It is Vladimir's probing of Pozzo that finally brings the former's great outburst about time and the transience of the human condition. The dumb Lucky and the blind Pozzo leave the stage, and all we have as a memory of them is the sound of yet another fall that leaves them waiting off-stage for whoever may be willing to come to their aid.

A Boy

There may be one Boy, two Boys, or an infinite series of them stretching back or extending forward until Godot arrives. Towards the end of Act 1 a Boy makes his timid entrance on to the stage. He has evidently been expected, since Estragon asks him what has kept him so late. He appears to have been waiting uncertainly for some time, and the suggestion is that he has been frightened of Pozzo and Lucky, the whip and the noise.

Vladimir eventually tries to pin down the Boy's identity as the same one who had been there the previous day. He denies this, and says that this is his first visit. The lad delivers his message in a burst of words, and promises faithfully that Godot will be coming the next day. Vladimir cross-questions him about his relationship with Godot and about his own occupation. He appears to be the goat-herd, while his brother looks after the sheep. He is Godot's favourite, as it is his brother who seems to get the beatings. He has genuine doubts of his own happiness, but accepts his state of life. The message he has to take back to Godot concerns the actual existence of the two tramps. He has seen them, hasn't he? Then that is the message he must carry to Godot.

In Act 2 a Boy enters evidently seeking Vladimir, whom he addresses as 'Mr Albert' (as also in Act 1, p.49). Although he recognizes the tramp, he seems not to be the same Boy as the messenger of the previous day. Vladimir questions him about Godot, and it transpires that Godot does not actually *do* anything; and that he has a beard, possibly white. Vladimir expresses deep concern at the second piece of information with a heartfelt cry (p.92). Once again the message to be carried back to Godot concerns the existence of the two tramps and the reality of the meeting with the Boy. The lad finally eludes the lunge Vladimir makes at him, and runs off into the night.

The nameless ones

These characters, like Godot, never appear on stage, but we have the feeling that they are not far away throughout the action.

At the start of Act 1 we hear that they have beaten Estragon, and that they have done this before.

In Act 2, after Estragon has again been parted from Vladimir, we hear that he has once more been beaten. He now numbers his assailants, and says that there were ten of them. Truth being at something of a premium in this play, we are at liberty either to accept or reject this number of attackers. Perhaps, like Falstaff at the Gadshill ambush, a monstrous regiment has grown out of two men. But at any rate, a specific number is mentioned, and an exact incident suggested. Such accuracy is rare in the play, and is thus worthy of note. We hear of these assailants once again, when Vladimir is urging Estragon to attack Lucky. He reminds him that it was Lucky who had kicked him the previous day, to which Estragon replies, 'I tell you there was ten of them' (p.79). But even with the odds at two to one, Vladimir needs the victim to be asleep before he can consider the possibility of success.

Themes and structure

Themes

Beckett has said that he finds drama relaxing for him: 'You have a definite space and People in this space. That's relaxing.' Within the confines of the stage he is able to touch on a number of themes without necessarily coming to any conclusion about them. He leaves each of us to work out our own conclusion. The plan of the play is cyclical, and we keep returning to our starting-point. This idea is echoed in Vladimir's song at the beginning of Act 2, in the mournful dirge that could go on for ever about the death of a dog whose saga is perpetuated on its tombstone for all the other dogs to read *ad infinitum*. It is the same theme as we find in T. S. Eliot (in the first line of 'East Coker'): 'in my beginning is my end', and nowhere do we find it more powerfully expressed than in the 'birth over a grave' image later in the play.

Repentance and salvation

Vladimir sees hope for them in repentance for sin. Estragon, however, sees their only fault as that of having been born. The guffaw with which Vladimir greets this statement is swiftly stifled, and his face becomes a mask of emotions that are turned on and off at will. Estragon, the cynic, constantly stops Vladimir in his tracks as he demands explanations of self-evident terms like 'Saviour' and 'Hell'. Yet, as we have said, it is he who dismisses general opinion as not being worthy of attention.

Neither tramp is able to seek salvation from a position of strength. They are abject creatures putting forward 'A vague supplication', and on their hands and knees at that. They are also constantly afraid, and when they think Godot is coming they huddle together for comfort.

There is a kind of lottery about their hopes of salvation. All four writers of the Gospels had witnessed the Crucifixion, yet only one mentioned the salvation of one of the thieves. Vladimir takes this as significant, while Estragon dismisses it as a vagary of the Gospel writer. They do, however, accept the odds of being saved as quite high. After all, one of the thieves was saved, and there are two of them. Perhaps their fear and reluctance to break off their friendship depends on this. They may be loath to risk discovering which of them is to be saved.

Time

Time and its passing is a recurrent topic in the conversation of the tramps. The hours are tedious until Godot comes, but they must be passed somehow. Talk is called for, and an element of intellectual discussion. The pressing needs of nature are attended to, and this gives the illusion of action – something is being achieved. Food is a palliative and a further time-killer. It can be discussed, and the merits of one root vegetable set against another. Pozzo and Lucky create a diversion, which sets the tramps off on further lines of thought to beguile them in their interminable wait. It is in fact Pozzo who in the first Act rejects Vladimir's charge 'Time has stopped', as he listens to the ticking of his watch and so refutes this blasphemy. Although Vladimir points out that the hours are long, there is some hope; as he remarks in Act 2, p.77.

Meanwhile there are further pastimes. The tramps can mime the episode of Pozzo and Lucky; they can re-enact it in fantasy. They can also revile one another in bitter invective, rising (or stooping) to the final insult: 'Crritic!' But this has gone too far even for Vladimir, as we hear of his dismay and read the stage-direction *He wilts, vanquished, and turns away.* All the characters in the play are vague about when yesterday was and when tomorrow will be. Was it really 'a million years ago, in the nineties' when the then presentable pair, Vladimir and Estragon, might have hurled themselves to destruction from the top of the Eiffel Tower? Will they really come back tomorrow, and will that morrow see Godot's arrival?

Place

The tramps are constantly trying to identify their rendezvous. There is repeated doubt about whether they are at the right spot or not. It is through an attempt at such identification that we find the only visible symbolic change in the play – the sprouting of the leaves on the tree. This latter is the only obvious prop on stage when we meet the two tramps, and it is quickly drawn to our notice. There is a crisis of identity about it, as to whether it is a tree, a bush, alive or dead, and even what kind of tree it is. The idea of place is vague as far as the two are concerned, and they will not commit themselves to any accurate identification. Vladimir puts it into words with his angry 'Nothing is certain when you are about.' Throughout the play directions are given in either a flippant or solicitous tone, while the static and inactive is emphasized:

Pozzo 'I don't seem able . . . (*long hesitation*) . . . to depart.'

In the second Act Vladimir taunts Estragon with his inability to remember and to recognize their location; this rouses him to the bitter rejoinder, 'What is there to recognize? All my lousy life I've crawled about in the mud!' (p.61). As the conversation continues, and the sprouting of leaves on the tree causes comment, Estragon refutes the fact that they have ever been there before, and Vladimir seizes eagerly on this one point of agreement. It is the presence of the boots, however, that causes further doubt, but are they really Estragon's boots? Determined to orientate themselves, Vladimir theorizes about the footwear and reaches the (for him) satisfactory conclusion that that was where Estragon had been sitting the previous evening. It is another item of clothing, however, that clinches the identification of place, namely Lucky's hat. There is no gainsaying that monstrosity, and hope once more dawns.

Night and the dark

The coming of night with the attendant suggestion of oblivion is one of the play's most frequent allusions. Vladimir asks repeatedly if night will never come, Pozzo says that if he had their task he would wait till it was black night before he gave up, and there is the sinister overtone, 'But night does not fall.'

This is a twilight play; it could not face the full glare of noon. Act 1 has the laconic setting, *A country road. A tree. Evening.* Act 2 could not be more precise or repetitive – *Next Day. Same time. Same Place.* It is night with its suggestion of release, or at least rest, that the two tramps seek, and it is this as well as the arrival of Godot that they await. Vladimir links the two ideas in Act 2 with the entrance of Lucky and the blind Pozzo. Feeble as the two are, he sees them as reinforcements, and knows that somehow their presence will ensure the survival of Estragon and himself. The company of other humans means that they 'are no longer alone, waiting for the night ... It's tomorrow.' But, of course, it is not. They are still chained to circumstance, unable to move far, and with dawn stifled in its birth.

Food

Estragon never quite gets what he asks for the first time. A carrot is mysteriously transformed into a turnip and angrily rejected, but in the end the desired food is discovered and the carrot produced. The longer he eats it, however, the worse the taste is, but Vladimir asserts the contrary. When Pozzo and Lucky appear later in the same Act, much is made of the preparations for the picnic and Pozzo's evident enjoyment of it. There is nothing jaded about Estragon's appetite. He is ravenous, and overcomes his normal timidity to satisfy his craving for the discarded chicken bones. There is an irony in Vladimir's scandalized remark to this (p.27).

Immediate things like the need for food brook no delay and need instant remedy, even at the expense of good manners and decorum. *Those who have waited so long for Godot must have basic desires met more swiftly.*

In the second Act we have the same charade over the eating of the radish. The search for food implies action, and Estragon accepts the black and uninviting radish rather than going to seek the carrot he would prefer.

Part of Vladimir's function in the play, therefore, seems to be as provider for his friend. He may not be able to offer food that is always to Estragon's liking, but at least he is able to nourish Estragon's body to some extent, as he does his mind in the endless points for debate he offers him.

Sleep and dreams

In the play sleep is denied Estragon almost as a form of torture. He is constantly settling down and being prodded into wakefulness by Vladimir. It is as though sleep, like death, implies a separation, and this neither of them can bear. Right at the start of the play Vladimir has asked, 'May one enquire where His Highness spent the night?', and there is a gap filled by sleep between the two acts. As well as being an escape from reality, sleep allows the tramps to dream. The dreams, however, must remain private, as Vladimir will have no share in them. He shouts at the top of his voice in a kind of terror, 'DON'T TELL ME.'

In the second Act Estragon finds the effort of trying to remember too much for him, and complains that he is tired. But he is forced into attention as Vladimir points out the leaves on the tree that have grown in the time he has slept. In the muddle of bodies on stage after the blind Pozzo has fallen and they all become hopelessly entangled, Estragon's solution is to have a snooze – and they do, indeed, fall asleep.

Later, when Pozzo and Lucky have made their final exit, Estragon once more takes comfort in sleep but, as usual, this is short-lived. Vladimir wakes him, and Estragon asks him bitterly why he will never allow him to sleep. Once again the excuse for Vladimir's action is his loneliness, and again he refuses to listen to Estragon's dream. It is Vladimir, however, who is left to consider the whole theme of reality as opposed to the dream state: 'Was I sleeping, while the others suffered? Am I sleeping now?' Desperately he tries to establish the truth of his situation, yet he cannot bear the conclusion to which his thoughts are leading him.

Suffering

Throughout the play there is the contrast between physical and spiritual suffering.

The sight of the running sore on Lucky's neck horrifies the tramps. This sign of his servitude causes them great concern, but with their usual attitude of acceptance they take it as inevitable. The contrast is thus so much the greater when they turn on Lucky and revile him for his treatment of Pozzo. Sympathy for Pozzo is in its turn short-lived, and his: '... and now ... he's killing me' is lost in his speech of recovery:

(*calmer*) 'Gentlemen. I don't know what came over me ...'

It is the same character, remember, who is later begging for help in piteous tones as he grovels on the ground without the aid of his dumb menial. The tramps too have physical disabilities. Vladimir, with his weak bladder and hint of more serious disease, and Estragon with his painful feet, are constantly referring to their ailments.

Estragon especially has his share of receiving and giving pain. His attempt to be kind to Lucky is repaid by a kick on the shin. In Act 2, when the situation is different, Estragon has a chance of taking his revenge. In the event, however, it is he who suffers yet again (p.88).

There is no doubt, however, that in comparison even with the tramps, Lucky and Pozzo suffer the greater privations. Lucky is bereft of speech and Pozzo of sight, although the latter still retains his authority in spite of this. Suffering has to be endured. There is no escape for any of the characters in the play. On each occasion that it is suggested the tramps reject the idea of suicide. Neither sees any hope of success that way, and the notion is reduced to the level of farce with the falling of Estragon's trousers through lack of the rope that might have brought release from torment.

Biblical themes and references

From the opening gambit of Vladimir's account of the Crucifixion the play abounds in religious references and biblical imagery. The Bible is central to the meaning of the play.

On stage we have two creatures who, late in the action, are able to assert: 'We are men.' The audience is constantly being told that they are made in God's image, and these two scarecrows even have the effrontery to liken themselves to Christ:

Vladimir: But you can't go barefoot!
Estragon: Christ did.

Estragon hints at this idea too when he says in reply to Vladimir's taunt:

Estragon: The best thing would be to kill me, like the other.
Vladimir: What other? (*Pause.*) What other?'

But Estragon will not be drawn. The Cross itself is an image that is used in at least two tableaux in the play, and is a frequent point of reference. Vladimir berates Lucky for his treatment of Pozzo (a total reversal of the master/servant situation): 'Such a good master! Crucify him like that!'

The idea of Christ on the Cross flanked by the two malefactors is taken up in Act 1 immediately after Lucky's long tirade. First we have the tableau of Lucky, supported by Estragon and Vladimir, then the stage direction *Vladimir and Estragon hoist Lucky to his feet, support him an instant, then let him go. He falls.*

We find the direct antithesis of this scene in Act 2, only this time it is Pozzo they are supporting. Then follows the significant stage direction *Pozzo sags between them, his arms round their necks.*

In each situation we have a reminder of the scene at Calvary, and in each case the tramps are set in supporting roles to the main protagonist.

The basic theme of waiting is itself supported by a text from the Book of Proverbs, 13, 12: 'Hope deferred maketh the heart sick, but when the desire cometh it is a tree of life', and as we have already remarked, the tree in the second part of the play has four or five leaves. To Vladimir at least this is a sign of hope.

There is no denying the fact of the tree's sprouting, even though there may be exaggeration in the extent of its foliage. One other biblical reference is worthy of note. The tramps return to the word-magic of proper names. This is the same game as that played by Ulysses in the cave of the Cyclops when he concealed his identity under the disguise of Noman, to the subsequent confusion of the giant. In Act 2, when Pozzo is down and at their mercy, they taunt him and cast further doubts on his identity:

Vladimir: I tell you his name is Pozzo.
Estragon: We'll soon see . . . Abel! . . . Perhaps the other is called Cain . . .'

The terrible significance of the universality of the character should not be lost to us in Estragon's 'He's all humanity.'

Nor can we fail to hear in the whole play Cain's reply to God's question after the murder of his brother Abel: 'Where is thy brother Abel?' And he said, 'I know not: Am I my brother's keeper?' (Genesis, 4, 9.) Nor is Abel's punishment unlike that of the ever-wandering Pozzo and Lucky: 'A fugitive and a vagabond shalt thou be in the earth.' His acceptance of the situation is also like that of these two itinerants: 'I shall be a fugitive and a vagabond in the earth, and it shall come to pass, that every one that findeth me shall slay me.'

Structure

No matter how vague our notions may be, we all have some idea of what to expect from a dramatic performance. Many of us have been brought up on the pattern of plays showing the development of character; we have been stimulated by novel situations and kept interested by twists of plot. Poetry and music

have effectively enlivened the duller moments of some plays for us –
Shakespeare was a master of such devices. What then, with such a
tradition behind us, are we to make of *Waiting For Godot*? It will help
if we adopt the same approach that we need for the reading of
modern poetry. Here too a long tradition teaches us what to expect.
We look eagerly for rhyme, fixed metrical arrangement, rhythm,
predictable stresses, but we frequently look in vain. In order to
understand and appreciate this work a new conception of the
nature and potential of poetry is essential. If we approach drama
from a similar standpoint we can at least begin to understand
Waiting For Godot more fully. What T. S. Eliot did for 20th-century
poetry in *The Waste Land*, Samuel Beckett did for the modern
theatre in this play.

Waiting For Godot was first produced in Paris in 1953; then in
London in 1955. Mystified audiences tried to unravel the puzzle;
the author himself forecast that it would play to empty houses.
Indeed, Beckett's secret hope that such would be the case may be the
key to understanding his motives in writing the play. In the event,
however, *Waiting For Godot* was hugely successful. From its first
performance it has attracted a spate of critics and interpreters;
countless producers have added their ideas to presentation. We in
turn have to consider how a play in which so little happens can hold
audiences for three hours and send them home still discussing the
experience. A recent television showing in America evoked the
comment from one fireside critic: 'It was a play about two tramps in
a desert and nothing happened.' This echoed a more serious and
scholarly critic, Eva Metman, who suggested that the story concerned 'two tramps who dawdled in a barren place awaiting a
rescuer from misery.' If we are looking for a story we are going to be
disappointed; we must therefore be prepared to revise any precon-
ceived notions we may have about what constitutes a play.

The boy in Act 2, who claims to be on his first visit to the tramps,
addresses Vladimir as Mr Albert, just as the first boy took similar
liberties with his identity. Within the pairs of characters we find the
same balance. Vladimir is the incurable romantic, always harking
back to the golden days. Estragon concerns himself with the
moment, yet cannot cope with immediate events. The relationship
between the two tramps is one of intimacy, and they have been
likened to a long-married couple who have grown so used to each
other that they are too apathetic to bring their partnership to an
end.

In Pozzo and Lucky we have the more formal situation of master and servant, with the traditional trappings of reward and punishment maintaining domination and subservience. The image of the rope used to bind Lucky is transferred in function to hold up Estragon's trousers, with frequent allusions to its more sinister possible use as a hangman's noose.

Beckett has been rightly praised for the symmetry of his work, and however inconsequential the dialogue of *Godot* may sound, the construction of the play has a definite pattern. There is a balance in each of the two Acts, and each Act complements the other. The tramps, Vladimir and Estragon, talk; Pozzo and Lucky enter and join the conversation; on their departure the Boy appears with the news that Godot won't be coming that day.

Act 2 follows this pattern, the significant difference being that Pozzo is now blind and Lucky dumb. The only change in the scenery throughout is that in Act 2 we are told that the tree has sprouted four or five leaves.

Style

Vladimir and Estragon may look like tramps, but the topics they range over, and the smattering of foreign and classical languages they use, show them to be well above the level of most itinerant dropouts.

Beckett makes use of a rapid interchange between them that carries us forward with its pace; short, sharp speeches of the nature of *stichomythia*, which apparently do not advance the action but add detail to detail until the topic is exhausted. We find this first in Act 1, when they are discussing the fate of the thieves at the crucifixion (p.13):

Estragon: What's all this about? Abused who?
Vladimir: The Saviour.
Estragon: Why?
Vladimir: Because he wouldn't save them.
Estragon: From hell?
Vladimir: Imbecile! From death.
Estragon: I thought you said hell.
Vladimir: From death, from death.

In this short exchange we have the idea of salvation and the equation of death and hell.

The Irishness of the tramps is brought out on occasion by the use of specifically Irish terms, although the two of them can be played as natives of Ireland throughout. Quite near the start of the play Estragon says, 'Stop blathering and help me off with this bloody thing.' (Act 1, p.10.) The word 'blather', or 'blether', is used frequently in Ireland and Scotland for the empty chattering that is likened to a bladder of wind. Indeed, the inflatable part of a football is still called a 'blether' in parts of Scotland.

Beckett, however, is not tempted to let the Irishness of the dialogue take over. He uses the nature of his countrymen, but is not prepared to submerge his message in their language. French, in which he was writing, imposed a discipline that left no room for the whimsical Irishry of a Synge or an O'Casey.

He is not averse, however, to poking fun at both the English and the French, as when Estragon says 'Calm ... calm ... The English say *cawm*' – a line that is guaranteed to win a laugh from any audience. When the tramps are asked their opinion of Pozzo's speech about the night it is Vladimir who first catches the implication of his 'How did you find me?' with his answer 'Oh very good, very very good.' But from Estragon Pozzo wins the typically British Tommy's mock-French 'Oh tray bong, tray tray tray bong'. Every now and again we are reminded of the Irish speech rhythms and vocabulary. When the boy appears we hear him say, 'I mind the goats, sir.' with its idea of watching over the flocks and a link with biblical language.

Throughout the play there are Latin tags gleaned from the law and the philosophers. *Qua* – meaning 'as' or 'in the nature of' features prominently among these, and is found in Lucky's long speech, both for sound in a repetitive way as well as for legal overtones. When the blind Pozzo ponders his loss of sight Estragon urges him to say more of his deprivation. Vladimir bids him leave the man in peace because he is 'thinking of the days when he was happy'.

Comedy and stage business

The tramps have been likened to Laurel and Hardy by some critics, and to Charlie Chaplin by others. Perhaps there is something of the circus clown added for good measure. Much of the 'business' Beckett makes them enact is part of the stock-in-trade of the lighter side of the theatre. Boots will always be associated with Charlie Chaplin: there was even a song composed about his footwear. So, if the borrowing from the cinema is authentic, it is not strange to find Estragon fumbling with his boots right from the start of the play. The bowler hat also was part of the wardrobe of these three film comedians, and it featured widely in many of their gags. Its distinctive shape, and the uses to which it could be put, make it an easy object of ridicule.

Beckett uses the protracted joke as part of his technique, and this too has been borrowed from comedians like Laurel and Hardy. Part of the charm (or irritation, depending on one's point of view) of their jokes was to be found in their repetitive nature and their predictability. A piano being delivered up a flight of steps finally made it to the top, before immediately hurtling down to its starting-point. We find a similar situation with the business of the hat being passed from one to the other in Act 2; there are twenty-four lines of stage-directions describing the sequence in the transfer of Lucky's hat from Vladimir to Estragon.

The arrival of Pozzo and Lucky gives additional scope for stage techniques borrowed from pantomime and burlesque. Lucky, as the one-end-of-the-ladder joke (though in this case it is a rope), is well across the stage before Pozzo appears. Just as their arrival is unexpected, so we are eager to know who is dominating this strangely cowed creature. The whip, symbol of authority, leaves us in no doubt about the relationship of the two. This domination is completed by the ballet of the picnic and the staccato parade-like orders barked out by the autocratic Pozzo to the robot-like Lucky. The overloaded servant has been part of the comedy scene since clowns first made their appearance. Here, however, it is the logical nature of the dropping and retrieving that adds to the effect. The precision is the same as that we find in the coke-stealing scene in Wesker's *Chips with Everything*. This is a skilfully planned piece of business, and no haphazard falling about. Later in the second Act we have the splendid knock-about comedy of Vladimir trying to look at Estragon's leg (p.67).

Shortly after, there is a weird miming of the Pozzo and Lucky scene, with its strange, 'venereal' cursing: 'Gonococcus! Spirochaete!' (The bacterium causing gonorrhoea and the spiral organism of syphilis.) This is a prelude to the arrival of the strangely changed pair, the one blind and the other dumb, so that the two scenes are linked by a contrived mime. Part of the pantomime ploy used is the hiding-place that fails to conceal, with the joke being shared by the audience. Vladimir pushes Estragon towards the auditorium as a way of escape, but he recoils in horror.

The only other place of concealment is the tree, and that proves of little use – either for suicide or as a hiding-place.

Tableaux and silence

As we have seen, the stage setting for the play is as stark as the dialogue and as simple as the props. All our attention is focused on the actors. Every action is significant in a play where there is comparatively little movement.

From the opening of the curtain on the first Act we have sight of the tramps in characteristically indolent attitudes. Estragon is sitting on a low mound, making heavy weather of removing one of his boots. The effort proves abortive, and he rests. Vladimir approaches with a wide-legged walk and takes up his stance on stage. The only movement is that of the tramps looking inside boot or hat for foreign bodies. When they do eventually move it is with some effort, and they do so with difficulty, looking into wings or auditorium as though in search of something. Vladimir seems the more agitated of the two, and he can't bear the ease with which Estragon finds escape in sleep. His own weak bladder causes him to make frequent and rapid exits out of sight of the audience to the side of the stage. Estragon is at hand to encourage him and to mime his actions.

Throughout the early part of the scene there have appeared the words 'Pause' and 'Silence' in the stage directions. It is as though a near-physical effort is needed to keep the dialogue going, and to elicit any kind of response from a partner.

Silence is used in a more positive fashion in the scene where the tramps thinks they hear Godot. So we have the two statues stiff with anticipation and their silence shared by the audience, which is only able to relax when they do.

It is this kind of silence that is contrasted with the stage direction 'A terrible cry, close at hand'; when eventually, not Godot, but Pozzo and Lucky appear.

The eventual conversation between the tramps and Pozzo also has its share of silences. Pozzo, however, does not seem to be embarrassed by them. The other two remain silent, and the attempt at interchange dies.

Pozzo himself is an adept at striking poses, particularly when he wants to attract and hold an audience. He uses his throat-spray to catch attention, as he has previously used the ritual of the filling and lighting of his pipe. He is the dominating figure in the tableau as they look at the sky.

Pozzo: A great calm descends. (*Raising his hand.*) Listen! Pan sleeps.

In violent contrast to such scenes we have the unleashed fury of Lucky's tirade and the frantic efforts of the rest to stifle him and restore peace once more.

The Act ends in the tableau of the tramps in silence, having decided to go but not moving.

The second Act continues the theme of silence.

In the dialogue between Vladimir and Estragon that follows there are significant stage directions: 'Silence' and 'Long Silence'. It is as though Beckett is making a stylized punctuation of the silences. This would seem to be in accord with the production at the Royal Court Theatre, supervised by the author and using his English text. Here the farcical element was played down, and the pathos of the last few moments in each act emphasized the more.

At the end of the play we have Estragon asleep and Vladimir interrogating the boy about the nature of Godot. After the lad runs off we have:

Silence ... Vladimir stands motionless and bowed.

It is this picture that we take with us as we leave the theatre.

Philosophy and meaning of the play

Philosophy

There is a danger of our becoming lost if we spend too much time in trying to probe the philosophy behind the work; Beckett does not acknowledge the influence of any one particular philosophy more than another. There is, however, a good deal of the mystic about the author, and this is reflected in his characters. He does, after all, take one of the central moments of the Christian belief, the Crucifixion, as a starting point in one of his philosophical digressions and, although the mystical approach may not always be specifically Christian, it can frequently be termed religious.

Since Beckett was writing in Paris, and in view of his play's date, it is not surprising that his ideas should be linked with those of Sartre and the philosophy with which he was associated, Existentialism. This was a way of thinking that moved counter to the traditional view of Plato. The Platonists believed that whatever was good and beautiful reflected a particle of the supreme goodness and beauty. In *Adonais* Shelley, writing of the dead Keats, suggests that he is now part of the loveliness which 'Once he made more lovely.' In other words, he is now one with the supreme essence. The Existentialists denied the existence of this supreme state, and said that eternal truths were illusion, and that it was for the individual to work out his own salvation. Experience was what counted, and its nature determined our characters. It was up to each of us, therefore, to seek our own identity.

If we look at the rest of Beckett's writing we find that this search for identity is a recurrent theme. In *Endgame* the father and mother in their dustbins look back to their lost youth, when they rode tandem on their honeymoon. Malone, in the novel *Malone Dies*, desperately seeks his identity as he lies dying. Perhaps, however, the theme is most obvious in *Krapp's Last Tape* as the hero listens to the tape of his youthful voice, whose message he fails to comprehend and which he is unable to identify.

There is no reason, therefore, to dismiss this theme of

Beckett's simply because the characters he chooses to delineate are at the lower end of human society. Their search for identity is as valid as our own, and their quest perhaps made more poignant by the depths they have plumbed.

Meaning

As with the interpretation of Godot himself, the author stead-fastly refused to be drawn into discussion over the meaning of the work. In 1956, however, he did hint that the great success of the play had been due to the fact that the public had insisted on 'imposing allegorical and symbolic meaning on a play which was striving to avoid definition'. One is tempted to ask what else he expected them to do, as without those imposed meanings we have a pretty incomprehensible farrago. Even with them appreciation of the work is not easy.

The first audiences in America were bewildered by the play, chiefly as it had been billed as the comedy hit of Europe. (Students will note that it is classed as 'A Tragicomedy in two Acts'.) The Americans were making for the exits in droves long before the interval. Those who stayed, however, might have realized that they were watching something very significant. As one critic suggested, 'Godot gave the theatre a new starting point.'

There have been as many interpretations of the play as there have been critics, and no doubt further theories will be added to the store as time goes on. Kay Boyle, for example, worked out an elaborate analogy between the play and Beckett's stay in France during the war. (His return to that troubled region was itself a kind of perversity.) She pointed to the end of the second act, with its reference to the Pyrenees, and likened that to the escape route used by the prisoners during the German occupation. Beckett himself said there wasn't a word of truth in it; though, as she adds 'He has never held that, or anything else, against me.'

At any rate, here is a play that we cannot ignore, interpret it as we may. The author, from his self-imposed isolation in Paris emerges to give instruction and advice to producers of the play, and no doubt every production adds a little more to our under-standing of its meaning. Beckett has pointed the way with his work, and we must follow as we can.

One interpretation of the play is the equation of Vladimir with the body, and Estragon with the mind; and the action of the one upon the other. Beckett himself recognized this duality (he calls it pseudocouple, the splitting of self). His reading of the philosophy of Arnold Geulincx (1624–69) encouraged him in this line of thought, and it is interesting for us to follow the links through to *Waiting For Godot*. Basically, the philosopher posits that the body and soul are distinct parts of our being, and that God has control only of the body. We are able to control our minds. The more perceptive among us consequently fall back on mental processes that we can manipulate for ourselves. The fact that the body can act under the mind's stimulus is explained by Geulincx in the terms of two clocks that synchronize while remaining independent. Colin Duckworth sees this as the reason for the tramps' inability to go to Pozzo's aid when he falls in Act 2. Their time-scale has got out of phase, and they are unable to carry out the simplest physical movement.

General questions

1 What dramatic use does Beckett make of techniques derived from the circus and music-hall? (Suggestions on how to tackle this question appear at the end of this section.)

2 Show how Beckett was concerned with man as 'a lonely and impotent creature in a hostile universe' in this play.

3 'Beckett's world is a hostile world.' Discuss.

4 Consider Beckett's treatment of Time in this play.

5 What difficulties would you consider might face a producer of *Waiting for Godot*?

6 Contrast the roles of Vladimir and Estragon in the play.

7 'Let us do something while we have the chance.' Develop this idea as you find it in the play.

8 'He's all humanity.' How closely does this in fact relate to Pozzo?

9 What is Lucky's role in the play?

10 What is the function of the Boy in each of the Acts?

11 'Although he never appears, Godot serves a vital purpose in the play.' Discuss.

12 Would you prefer to read this play or see it acted? Give reasons for your answer.

13 What do you think was behind Beckett's hope that *Waiting for Godot* would play to empty houses?

14 Write an essay on the stage devices used in the play, e.g. the business of the hats; Lucky and his luggage; the tree; whip; stool etc.

15 Write a comparison of the two Acts of the play.

16 Try to account for the bewilderment felt by some of the early audiences when confronted by the play, saying what you yourself find difficult in it.

17 In what ways is the term tragi-comedy a definition of the play? Give reasons for your answer.

18 'Beckett's play abounds in religious imagery and thought.' Discuss.

19 'Godot remains off-stage, a mysterious and dwindling source of hope.' Do you find any hope in the play?

20 'Nothing to be done' is the message of *Waiting for Godot*. Do

you agree? Is this a nihilistic, totally pessimistic play?

Suggestions for answering Question 1

'What dramatic use does Beckett make of techniques derived from the circus and music-hall?'

Introduction
Pick out the key words and deal with them right away, making it clear how you are going to tackle them. The words here placed in a prominent position are, clearly, 'dramatic use'. 'Dramatic' is often used very loosely in questions, so make it clear how you understand it. At its basic level the word means 'in the drama'; 'in the action of the play'. How do the *techniques* specified add to the progress of the action? Are they an integral part of it or mere diversion? Here we are beginning to go more deeply into the idea of 'dramatic', this being now linked with the unity involved in character and stage-action.

Introduction
Leave 10 to 15 lines blank so that you may return and work at what is perhaps the most important part of the answer.

Paragraph 1, CIRCUS
(a) Make-up of Vladimir and Estragon. Tramps or clowns? Remember French theatre and use of mime. Little scenery in Circus – dependence on stage-props only. Estragon's boot – linked with clown's outrageous footwear. Falling about of Vladimir and Estragon as they think they hear the sound of a horse.
(b) Lucky and Pozzo. Circus animal and trainer. Clowning use of props – basket, whip, stool and rope. Much use is made of the ringmaster's whip.
(c) Lucky's sore place. Clown hiding tears and pain etc. Lucky's weeping when Pozzo suggests getting rid of him. Pathos of the clown.
(d) Pozzo – removing of hat to reveal total baldness. Shock – rather like all-white, hairless make-up of clown.

We could link these ideas with the remarks made by Vladimir and Estragon themselves.

V: It's worse than the pantomime.
E: The circus.
V: The music-hall.
E: The circus. (NB Repetition of 'circus'.)

(e) Lucky's performance. Like a puppet – do we want him to dance, to sing or to recite? These aptitudes are dismissed for hearing him think. Then there is his tirade like the mock oration of a clown to his audience.

(f) Pratfalls and trouser-dropping.

Paragraph 2, MUSIC-HALL
Effects are visual and verbal

VISUAL   (i) Contrast in physique between Vladimir and Estragon and the corpulent Pozzo and emaciated Lucky.

               (ii) Repetition. Stage-business with hats, boots and searching of clothing. Max Wall has related on television how he introduced arm-juggling into the business of the hat.

VERBAL   (i) 'Are you friends?' asks the blind Pozzo in Act 2. Estragon is convulsed but Vladimir clarifies, 'No, he means friends of his.'

               (ii) Long-winded elucidation of some problem, ostensibly for the benefit of the other partner, but, in fact, for the audience, e.g. the effect of the weight of the pair of them were they to use the tree from which to hang themselves.

               (iii) The Monologue. A great part of Victorian vaudeville. Lengthy speeches are made direct to the audience by all the characters.

               (iv) Verbal repetitions. Phrases repeated after long intervals of dialogue.
'Ah! That's better!' spoken by Pozzo and Estragon throwing into contrast the difference between their meals.

               (v) Suspense. We wait for several pages of dialogue before we have any kind of answer to Estragon's question to Pozzo of, 'Why doesn't he put down his bags?'

               (vi) The interweaving of two conversations bearing no relation to each other, e.g. the speech on page 39 introduced by Pozzo with the words, 'Gentlemen, you have been . . . civil to me.'

General points for conclusion
[In your plan it is as well to write down the word 'Conclusion' to remind yourself that the answer must be rounded off and not left limply in mid-air.]

Circus-cum-music-hall atmosphere superimposed on everyday conversation.

One-liners. Apparently friends of Suzanne and Beckett were amazed by how much the dialogue of the play echoed the conversation of the pair.

Straight man and feed are interchangeable. Estragon and Vladimir adjust to their roles as the one or the other.

Feet – Beckett always had trouble with his own. His walk has a curious lurching action about it – rather like that of Chaplin's tramp.

Hats – Marx brothers. Beckett adamant about the hats being bowlers – as worn by his father. Laurel and Hardy.

Among the differences between Act 1 and Act 2 is the fact that the cross-talk becomes more intellectual as the play progresses.

Some useful critical quotations

I'd be quite incapable of writing a critical introduction to my own works. Beckett

I have been brooding in my bath for the last hour and have come to the conclusion that the success of *Waiting for Godot* means the end of the theatre as we know it. Robert Morley

Waiting for Godot is 'about' two destitutes hopefully awaiting the promised arrival of a third, and not daring to move in case they miss him. The idea that Beckett is a uniformly depressing writer is a misconception. Martin Esslin (see *Further reading* over page)

He is uplifting, exhilarating in the theatre. For an actor, to explore his compassion and his lyricism is very satisfying. Jack MacGowran

He [Beckett] strips his figures so thoroughly of all those qualities in which the audience might recognize itself that to start with, an alienation effect is created that leaves the audience mystified. Dr Metman

Play architecture as it was understood by the writer of the well-made play . . . has given place to a seemingly abstract void in which plot, or dramatic story-telling, is almost non-existent. Hugh Hunt

The theatre of the absurd is 'a theatre of situation as against a theatre of events in sequence'. Martin Esslin (see *Further reading* over page)

For the pattern is desperate and yet the movement, paradoxically, hopeful; the feeling is bitter and dark, yet the speech lively, irrepressible; in an essential way comic and accepting. It is then not that the pattern cancels the movement, or the tone the feeling; it is just their tension that is the real action, the real language of the play. Raymond Williams on *Waiting for Godot* (see *Further reading*).

Further reading

En Attendant Godot, ed. Colin Duckworth (Harrap, 1966)
Original French text of play with 100 page introduction in English.

A Biography: Samuel Beckett, Deirdre Bair (Picador, 1980)

En Attendant Godot and *Fin de Partie*, ed. J. P. Little (Grant and Cutler Ltd, 1981)

Beckett: A Study of His Plays, John Fletcher and John Spurling (Eyre Methuen, 1972)

Samuel Beckett: A Collection of Critical Essays, ed. Martin Esslin (Prentice-Hall, New Jersey, 1966)

Samuel Beckett, John Pilling (Routledge and Kegan Paul, 1976)

A Reader's Guide to Samuel Beckett, Hugh Kenner (Thames and Hudson, 1973)

Drama from Ibsen to Brecht, Raymond Williams (Pelican Books, 1973)

Bouvard and Pécuchet, Gustave Flaubert; translation by A. J. Krailsheimer (Penguin Books, 1976)

Some other works by Beckett

Watt (John Calder, 1970)

Murphy (Picador, 1973)

Mercier and Camier (John Calder, 1977)

More Pricks than Kicks (Picador, 1977)

Company (Picador, 1982)

Pan study aids Titles published in the Brodie's Notes series

W. H. Auden Selected Poetry

Jane Austen Emma Mansfield Park Northanger Abbey Persuasion Pride and Prejudice

Anthologies of Poetry Ten Twentieth Century Poets The Poet's Tale The Metaphysical Poets

Samuel Beckett Waiting for Godot

Arnold Bennett The Old Wives' Tale

William Blake Songs of Innocence and Experience

Robert Bolt A Man for All Seasons

Harold Brighouse Hobson's Choice

Charlotte Brontë Jane Eyre

Emily Brontë Wuthering Heights

Robert Browning Selected Poetry

John Bunyan The Pilgrim's Progress

Geoffrey Chaucer (parallel texts editions) The Franklin's Tale The Knight's Tale The Miller's Tale The Nun's Priest's Tale The Pardoner's Tale Prologue to the Canterbury Tales The Wife of Bath's Tale

Richard Church Over the Bridge

John Clare Selected Poetry and Prose

Samuel Taylor Coleridge Selected Poetry and Prose

Wilkie Collins The Woman in White

William Congreve The Way of the World

Joseph Conrad The Nigger of the Narcissus & Youth The Secret Agent

Charles Dickens Bleak House David Copperfield Dombey and Son Great Expectations Hard Times Little Dorrit Oliver Twist Our Mutual Friend A Tale of Two Cities

Gerald Durrell My Family and Other Animals

George Eliot Middlemarch The Mill on the Floss Silas Marner

T. S. Eliot Murder in the Cathedral Selected Poems

J. G. Farrell The Siege of Krishnapur

Henry Fielding Joseph Andrews

F. Scott Fitzgerald The Great Gatsby

E. M. Forster Howards End A Passage to India
Where Angels Fear to Tread

William Golding Lord of the Flies The Spire

Oliver Goldsmith Two Plays of Goldsmith: She Stoops to Conquer;
The Good Natured Man

Graham Greene Brighton Rock The Power and the Glory
The Quiet American

Thom Gunn and Ted Hughes Selected Poems

Thomas Hardy Chosen Poems of Thomas Hardy
Far from the Madding Crowd Jude the Obscure
The Mayor of Casterbridge Return of the Native
Tess of the d'Urbervilles The Trumpet-Major

L. P. Hartley The Go-Between The Shrimp and the Anemone

Joseph Heller Catch-22

Ernest Hemingway For Whom the Bell Tolls
The Old Man and the Sea

Barry Hines A Kestrel for a Knave

Gerard Manley Hopkins Poetry and Prose of Gerard Manley Hopkins

Aldous Huxley Brave New World

Henry James Washington Square

Ben Jonson The Alchemist Volpone

James Joyce Dubliners A Portrait of the Artist as a Young Man

John Keats Selected Poems and Letters of John Keats

Ken Kesey One Flew over the Cuckoo's Nest

Rudyard Kipling Kim

D. H. Lawrence The Rainbow Selected Tales Sons and Lovers

Harper Lee To Kill a Mockingbird

Laurie Lee As I Walked out One Midsummer Morning
Cider with Rosie

Thomas Mann Death in Venice & Tonio Kröger

Christopher Marlowe Doctor Faustus Edward the Second

W. Somerset Maugham Of Human Bondage

Gavin Maxwell Ring of Bright Water

Thomas Middleton The Changeling

Arthur Miller The Crucible Death of a Salesman

John Milton A Choice of Milton's Verse Comus and Samson
Agonistes Paradise Lost I, II

Sean O'Casey Juno and the Paycock
The Shadow of a Gunman and the Plough and the Stars

George Orwell Animal Farm 1984

John Osborne Luther

Alexander Pope Selected Poetry

Siegfried Sassoon Memoirs of a Fox-Hunting Man

Peter Shaffer The Royal Hunt of the Sun

William Shakespeare Antony and Cleopatra As You Like It
Coriolanus Hamlet Henry IV (Part I) Henry IV (Part II) Henry V
Julius Caesar King Lear Love's Labour's Lost Macbeth Measure for
Measure The Merchant of Venice A Midsummer Night's Dream
Much Ado about Nothing Othello Richard II Richard III Romeo and
Juliet The Sonnets The Taming of the Shrew The Tempest Twelfth
Night The Winter's Tale

G. B. Shaw Androcles and the Lion Arms and the Man
Caesar and Cleopatra The Doctor's Dilemma Pygmalion Saint Joan

Richard Sheridan Plays of Sheridan: The Rivals; The Critic;
The School for Scandal

John Steinbeck The Grapes of Wrath Of Mice and Men & The Pearl

Tom Stoppard Rosencrantz and Guildenstern are Dead

J. M. Synge The Playboy of the Western World

Jonathan Swift Gulliver's Travels

Alfred Tennyson Selected Poetry

William Thackeray Vanity Fair

Flora Thompson Lark Rise to Candleford

Dylan Thomas Under Milk Wood

Anthony Trollope Barchester Towers

Mark Twain Huckleberry Finn

Keith Waterhouse Billy Liar

Evelyn Waugh Decline and Fall Scoop

H. G. Wells The History of Mr Polly

John Webster The Duchess of Malfi The White Devil

Oscar Wilde The Importance of Being Earnest

Virginia Woolf To the Lighthouse

William Wordsworth The Prelude (Books 1, 2)

William Wycherley The Country Wife

John Wyndham The Chrysalids

W. B. Yeats Selected Poetry